A collection of poems

Letters to my Beloved

Vindhya Goyal

ISBN
Paperback 979-8-89544-898-4
Hardcase 979-8-89556-255-0

To,
all those who live for love
and die for it every day

And to, my beloved
my husband

CONTENTS

PROLOGUE

Beloved.
One who is dear,
Very near to the heart.
Whom we adore, worship.
Who makes us feel,
As if we fall and
they rise every day
In love, which could be,
Of any sort,
feathers or swords
Fulfilled, ignored,
Maximised or shrunken,
Beloved, unaware of it.
Or completely absorbed,
In love like we do
From miles apart to
Sitting on the next chair,
Correct or wrong
Morally or ethically,

Faded or strong
Sleeping or awake
The love we hold
For our beloved is
Neither quantifiable,
Nor put under the laws.
Beloved is so dear
So near to the heart…

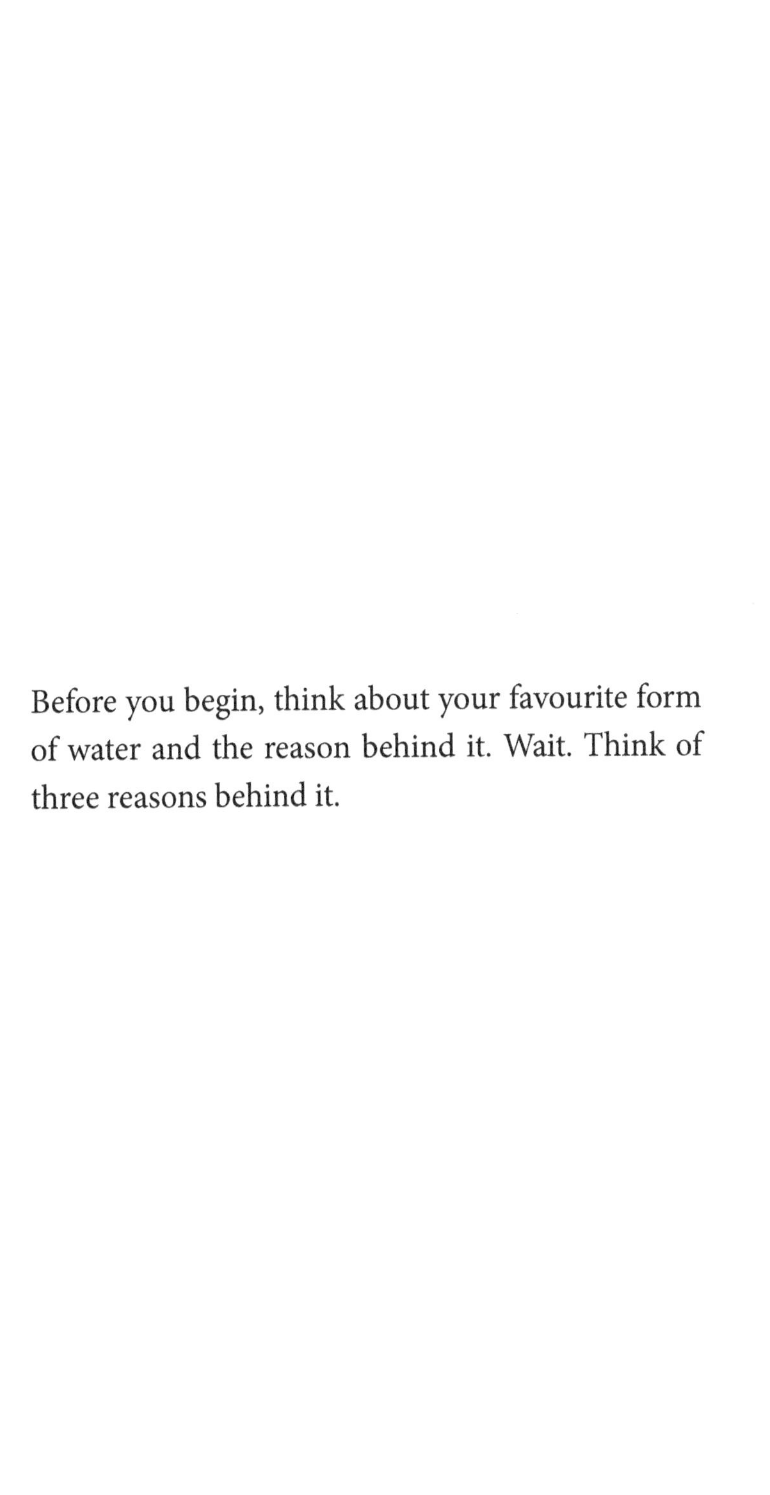

Before you begin, think about your favourite form of water and the reason behind it. Wait. Think of three reasons behind it.

HOW WAS THIS BOOK WRITTEN

Dear beloved,

I once read a relational psychology article, following which I asked you about your favourite form of water. It could have been anything: a glass of water, a river, or snow. From rainfall to glaciers, to even the water that gushes out of the nozzle of your shower, you could have answered anything. The significance of this question is related to the stories of our lives. I was obviously expecting you to ask me what my answer was going to be before you answered, so I was already prepared with it.

When I was a little kid, we used to live in a joint family in a big house of three floors with a lawn surrounding it. The terrace of that house reached an optimum height for us to see the river from it. The river was visible from the balcony too. I was always fascinated by it. From the time that I would wake up and go to school, to the time when I would return from there and go for riding my bicycle, the river seemed quite a constant object in my day-to-day life. Sometimes, I would just watch it from the terrace flow on and on. It would increase in volume as the monsoon would come to our part of the country.

As I grew, we shifted to a nuclear family in a smaller house in the same city. The river was still nearby. When I think of any form of water that would be dearest to me, it would be the river because it reminds me of my childhood. It was the thing that was constant throughout. The way I have turned out to become, the person that I am now, is all because of the thoughts that came into my mind when I was a kid. I realise now that the way my brain functions is because of all that I learnt in my childhood. You know, I overthink. That is something that has developed since the very beginning of my existence. I don't want to stop it. Reduce it? No, I don't want to reduce it. I want to overthink.

If you want me to elaborate, three reasons for it, then I would say:

1) The river is associated with my childhood, a time when I shaped my thoughts and dreamt of who and what I have become today. It was

a time when I fantasised about love and how it would be to fall in love with someone.

2) The river keeps flowing. Sometimes, when it would rain less, I would worry about the future. After ten to twenty years, it might dry all up because of no rain. But, turning back, I see it's been twenty years and it is still flowing. When I get too old, maybe fifty years from now, and I return to my childhood home just to summarise my life, it would still be there. The river would always connect me to the roots from where I had started dreaming.

3) I went to college in a nearby city where the same river flowed. It hasn't left me. Since the time of my birth, it has been there in my vicinity, just flowing forever.

Then, it was time for you to answer, and I know you don't think that much. You aren't someone who would see the poetic forms of incidences happening around you. But, I still wanted you to think and answer, if at all you were going to.

You said it would be the ocean.

The reasons you gave:

1) The ocean is vast. It's so huge that it's tough to mark where it starts and where it ends.

2) The ocean absorbs everything that you throw in it. Nothing could be as receptive as that. You throw a pebble, it would go down. You put a ship as large as the largest one built, it might sink it all.

You didn't have a third reason. Honestly speaking, I was satisfied even with one.

The significance of this question goes to the very inner aspects of one's personality - how one pictures love, how one wants love to be. The reasons that you thought for a particular form of water to be your favourite are the ways you want love to be, how you want to be loved. For instance, I have been very sensitive to both the inner and outer parts of my personality. Little things stay with me for years. I view love as something that would connect me to my roots right from the start. It has to be constant. It should be there even when it is hard to survive and even after knowing all about me. It should stay.

The way you see love is different. In fact, every person has a different approach to this question.

The more people, the more explanations. And more stories that form such beautiful answers. You want it to be vast, so that no one could contain it just in their hearts. It should be all over the body. One should not be able to start it and end it at the mere tips of their fingers.

You want it to be receptive. Love should absorb everything. Warmth. Wrath. Successes. Failures.

You didn't give me a third reason. I know you don't think that much. And I also know it isn't synonymous with, you don't care about me. You are just a practical person, unlike me who is a dreamy one. I think, actually firmly believe (after meeting you), that every dreamy person needs a practical partner to complete their lives.

The day we talked about all this, though it was very brief, but I had enough to analyse. I painted a small sketch for you. Maybe, just to give you another reason why you should love the ocean, because I sketched one for you. It had a boat in it, drawn with black coloured pens with nibs of variable thickness, travelling in the waves of the ocean that were haphazardly trying to reach the top of the boat. Love can seem like that at times, enraged as if it would drown us, but believe me, in the end, we all realise that love is never harsh. It's always better to fail in love rather than win by failing the other one. Here, I am with a third reason for you.

3) Ocean cures all the wounds. You remember all the times when we have been to the beach. Didn't it feel like therapy? Compared to the greatness of the waves that were flowing towards us and also away, our sorrows seemed so small, so tiny like a speck of dirt. Microscopic, I would say. This is how love should feel like. Like the ocean that cures all. All our sorrows are microscopic, almost nothing in front of love.

It was just a little question, a mere thought. But it helps us understand love better. Also, I am ready to complete all your answers. You just have to let me know where the initial point lies. Maybe there's no initial point, and there are just numerous points where we can touch each other. Where my descriptions for you would start and never end because the point where it stops would be the starting point of another description.

It was last month when I was cleaning my closet and found my old diaries. I started reading the poems I used to write before I met you. I am still petrified at how harshly I was traumatised by the wounds of love from my past. You just seem to have healed them all. There was a shift in the way I wrote then, and I write now."

FOREWORD

This book is a collection of poems about love, the rainbows, and the thunderbolts. In the beginning, you will find how each and every part of your beloved is dear to you. Moving towards the end, the parts still remain the same except for the fact that they have started hurting you. That's the difference between a lover and a beloved. A lover loves you back. But, a beloved is someone who may or may not acknowledge your love. These are poems written for your *beloved*. You don't know what would be the result of your love, but all you know is love.

Love is never ending. It doesn't have stops. No full stops. May be commas. May be too many question marks but, no full stops. You have to fall once, you will keep falling thereafter. The poems don't end here. They don't use full stops. Every action your beloved does, turns into the next line of your poem. How could such an emotion end? It could only pause to appreciate the beauty of your beloved but, never can it use a full stop

POEM. 1

FIRST SIGHT

(Beginning your day with their sight)

You are my favourite pair of eyes,
to look into with every sunrise.
As I get up as soon as I can,
by the touch of your hand
So, you might not think that
I'm still asleep and leave for work.
I don't move my hair falling.
On my face to behind my ears,
They cover my eyes, which watch
You smiling and making coffee.
Filling my heart with delight,
Stomach with magical butterflies,
It is the best part of my day, noon.
All the many minutes, evening, night.
Combined together, the best sight

POEM. 2

YOUR VOICE

(The first voice you hear in the morning)

Yes, little things matter.
That call, which ended
For ten simple seconds,
Mattered - made my day.
Reminded me of how you
Must have smiled, maybe.
Blushed in silence, maybe.
Sitting among other people,
Engrossed in heavy and
Meaningless discussions.

Hearing your soft voice,
Which, otherwise, is manly.
Heavier when you speak.
Your voice, the hushed one,
Mattered more than

Any syllable I heard,
Throughout the day, where
Dozens of people speak.
But what mattered was,
Your voice, as the sun rose,
From the eastern end,
As it rises every other day,
What matters is your voice

POEM. 3

DROPLET

(Mesmerised by Unintentional Behaviours)

How passionately I adore,
The tiny droplet of water,
That gets stuck in your beard.
Day after day, every day,
I keep staring at it keenly.
As you come for your,
Morning coffee on the couch.
After brushing your teeth,
Shining, when light falls on it.
And, I feel like catching it.
Within the pincer grasp,
My index finger and thumb.
Then, glide my palms over,
Your thick, black beard.
Pull your cheeks closer,
To my lips, gently place a kiss

That droplet is so tempting.
I wonder how you manage,
To get it there in your beard,
Day after day, every day.
Are you simply unaware of
It's sensuality, is it just a,
Matter of chance, or you
Know how tempting it is,
And manage to have it there.
In a seemingly unconscious,
But, totally intentional way?
What is the truth, you say?
Why is it always there
when you come after you brush?
That tiny droplet of water,
How badly I want to drown,
Myself, in it, how madly I
Want to pull you closer.
To my body, kiss your lips.
Day after day, every day

POEM. 4

BICYCLE

(Reliving the past with them)

On my way back from work,
I saw a bicycle this evening.
How smoothly it glided on.
Road of pebbles, all rough

And all the way back, I kept
Thinking of my childhood,
After completing homework,
I used to ride my bicycle.

I used to think of the future,
Never the past or present,
Just all the amazing things,
My life could turn out to be,

It was different from now.
I go to work on a scooter.
The lanes are a bit wider.
A bit more crowded, noisier.

But, I still think of the future.
Never, the past or present,
Some habits never change.
No matter how old you get,

The cycle rides were good.
But dreaming of you,
In my future, makes the
Scooter ones better.

Even when roads are, tortuous,
Scooter ones are better.
If you were to ask, what did
I dream of, while returning,

I would say I saw us cycling.
With the Sun about to set,
In a grassland far away,
Growing alongside a lake,

I saw us cycling. I know.
It's difficult to find a city,
It's difficult to hire two bicycles.
But, I would spare an evening,

An evening of our lives in a,
City far away, ride bicycle,
Next to you, dream together.
of a future, next to you

POEM NO. 5

DAWN

(Looking at you at dawn)

Early morning, when I look at your face,
Tan, and fresh with eyelids, a bit swollen
When I want to return to sleep but your,
Smile would not let me close my eyes.
Even when you say that you don't blush,
But, then you do, for a little while,
Just for a small second, after which you,
Realise you don't have to be shy because
You can enclose all expressions within
Not like me, who could not hide anything.
Not like an incomplete, handwritten diary.
In a language that you read with utmost,
Dexterity, effortlessly as if the diary is a
Bunch of letters meant to be mailed to you.
To a far land where you live without me.
Though you don't show, but even I know.

Oh, maybe I am just trying hard to know.
What you feel inside, and what you show
On your face that shines in sunlight, as you
Walk below huge banyan trees and the sun.
Rises above the horizon every morning.
When I see you just after waking up,
My day becomes all about the things,
We talk about at dawn, and your face
Flashes in front of my eyes, all the time

POEM. 6

DISTANCE

(Craving the touch of a distant beloved)

I have never met you,
never touched you,
with us sitting across
staring at each other
On screens, miles apart,
separate but wired
It still feels like I know
what your touch would,
Feel like on my bare flesh
And uncovered, barren skin

POEM. 7

WALLET

(Keeping the letters of love safe)

I thought, maybe, it would be
Kept in the corner of a room,
Where you sleep at night,
In the dark, when the moon shines,
Peeping through the glass.
Placed in wooden frames.
Which open on the balcony.
That hangs upon tall,
Green leafy palm trees.
Till your eyes could see,
I thought, maybe, it would be
Kept in the drawer,
The cabinet that stands,
Straight in the kitchen.
Where you listen to me.
Chirp like a bird while you

Make a warm Irish coffee.
Inside one of the jars,
Sugary things placed on,
Marble slab in alignment.
I thought, maybe, it would
Not be kept in a place that's
Safe enough to protect.
All the feelings that the
Words written on it had.
But, you kept it close in
The pocket of your wallet.
Where it would travel with you,
Wherever and whenever you go,
You'll find me, all of me in it

POEM. 8

HIDDEN CORRIDORS

(The meetings are momentary)

When I saw you today,
My mind stopped racing.
Everything just stopped.
Nothing else mattered.
More than talking to you
And watching you smile.
By pulling away, the
surgical mask on your lips
That covered your face.
Nothing else mattered.
More than pulling your
Warm hands from the
Deep pockets of your pants.
Which you wore flawlessly.

Rubbing your fingers,
Knowing it was momentary,
But, trying to find peace.
In the hidden corridors,
Where we would meet.
Hiding from the world

POEM NO. 9

STARRY EYES

(Waiting from a far place to meet)

I can't wait to lie down.
Quietly, by your side.
Staring at your starry,
Two bright little eyes

I have been counting the
Number of days on my
Fingers, which wait for
Your gentle, warm touch

To feel your arm below,
My head, like a pillow,
It is hard now; it aches.
To wait so much for you

Can't wait for you to come.
to the land near me, when
At just the view of you,
My heart would skip a beat

POEM NO. 10

ABOUT YOU

(Dreaming of living your life with them)

I saw you years ago,
Remember, in this land,
I dreamt of spending my
Entire life by your side.

You spoke a few words to me.
but, every move you made,
every word you uttered,
Was complete magic for me.

I dreamt of you in my sleep.
When awake, I thought,
But, I was unable to express
Let you know how I felt.

Years passed, and once more
I have come near you.
This time, a bit closer,
When can I say louder?

I know, I am optimum.
For you, all of your life.
And you are for me,
We are enough, optimum.

But, I am so hurt by the,
Sad endings of the past.
That I get frightened,
Sometimes, a few seconds

I know you are there.
Will always be here.
For us to create a lovely,
Immense, lovely family.

But, I overthink, and I get
too concerned at times,
Can't wait to start a life,
Where, together, we breathe.

We wake up and go to bed.
Together, breathe in air together.
Everything around me is about you
And around you is about me

POEM NO. 11

WAITING FOR YOU

(Craving for a long time)

I am ready to wait
For you to arrive
To hold me in your
Arms that fold around,
My waist wrapped up.
In blue satin laces.
To look into your eyes,
And then turn away
Breaking contact,
Only for you to
Bring me back,
Closer than ever before,
It, will be the first time,
I see you, feel you,
Smell you, touch you.

Ready to wait for it.
Even if you come
Late, after a while,
I am ready to wait

POEM NO. 12

SOUND OF MUSIC

(Dancing with your beloved)

With the sound of music,
Entering inside our ears,
Slowly, walking, vibrating.
Every little cell that could,
Not just hear, but feel.
Words being sung, echoing.
All through the stadium,
In all possible directions,
As I sink into your arms
Standing there in the middle
Oh! A thousand people,
All happen to be strangers.
But, I could only feel you.
Your arms encircling my waist,
And lips kissing me from behind.
On my unclothed, neck

Uncovered by the slow,
movement of your fingers,
Which gently remove hair locks,
Carelessly lying on my wet
Back and shoulders, but,
They have now reached home.
In the grip of your palms,
And we move just a little
To the sound of music,
Maintaining the touch,
Of our bodies and the notes,
That penetrate through us.
I sink deep down into
The endless layers of love.
With every passing moment,
I drown deeper and deeper.
My feet on the moist Earth.
Powerless, incapable of,
Swimming in the ocean,
Where I'm drowning, deeper

POEM NO. 13

MAKE YOU UP

(Making up from a distance)

I would come closer.
If I were near you
To hold your hands
To look into your
Eyes hidden behind
Rectangular frames
Then slowly, swiftly.
Put my palms tenderly,
On your warm cheeks,
That rarely, blush, red
But, I am a thousand.
Kilometres, maybe
A few more away
If I were near you
I would sing a song,
Lying down on bed

Light from the moon.
Falling on my face,
But I'm too shy for that,
Too concerned about the,
Notes that might get
Up, down, misplaced.
Looking at your face,
If I were there, near you
In your kitchen,
I would cook
Your favourite lunch.
Feed you with a spoon.
But, from here, I could
Only talk, make you imagine.
All that, I'll do when I come
And sit next to you.
Maybe lie down and
Make you up and
Make you realise
you look adorable
Even when you are
In, anger, in anguish,
But that doesn't mean
You will remain angry

POEM. 14

INTOXICATING SMILE

(Losing control by their smile)

The deep black T-shirt looks.
So Charming on you, like the,
Smile that arrives on your lips.
So tempting when we talk,
On your full lips, that I want to
Play with and look every day.
The way they move when you,
Are talking, listening, or smiling.
Or, even when you are furious,
I am confused about what suits more.
On you, that intoxicating smile,
Or, the black T-shirt you wore

POEM. 15

WHEN YOU ARRIVE

(Waiting to show them places you have visited
alone in the past)

Oh, what all I would do when you arrive
In my city, the lands where I grew up,
From a little girl dreaming of love, to this.
Day, when I am planning to show you.
All the places where I went on my bicycle.
Fallen flowers picked and hung from its basket.
That I used to collect through paths, which now
I want to walk with you, holding your hand.
May be curling up on one of your arms
As you keep smelling like a fresh autumn day,
And I want to take you to the bank of the river.
which I used to see daily, its waves, continuity,
Flowing effortlessly in the same direction
I want to visit the school where I studied
Temples, decorated and hidden deep inside,

Where I went strolling with my grandparents
Little shop where I got all artworks, framed
Standing at the side of a thin, crooked lane,
Roadside stall where I drank fruit squashes
With my brother or in a congested showroom.
From where I got hairbands with my sister,
All these places are still intact, but older.
Carrying golden memories of the past,
I want to tell you everything with details.
Things that I have loved, ones that I've craved,
But, I think I would just keep looking at you.
just keep looking at you when you are near,
Breathing the same air as you, in and out.
When you are here in the city where I grew,
Just keep feeling the warmth of your skin.
Take you on a tour of my city as you pull me,
From the deeper parts of your eyes, where
I'm drowning, unknowingly, lifelessly.
How to swim or pull myself out of them?
All the things I have described are just
A few written words forming phrases
What I have to show and share couldn't fit
And I would need more letters, definitely.
More ink and papers, as you give me
The feeling I could compose poems about

POEM. 16

MY HOME

(Searching for a home in a person)

Do you know that feeling?
When you enter your home,
Feel charged once again.
Even when you've been
Very tired, the air that you,
Inhale inside your room.
Brings you back to an
Unstoppable, happy life.
Such a peaceful place,
Whenever you reach home,
It gives you a feeling of,
Starting all over again.
Do you know, I want?
You need to be that person.
To whom I can always turn,
To feel like my home

POEM. 17

OUR HOME

(Building a home together)

Just the way I have painted,
Maybe with larger walls,
Windows that have beautiful,
Wildflower painted on curtains.

I want to live in a warm house
Which is sweet and delightful.
Standing on the outskirts of a city,
Where not many people reside

So that we can listen to songs
Of birds who visit us at dawn,
In the porch where we snuggle,
To have a cup of warm coffee

Eat Cookies that were crispier.
But have melted into our mouths.
We break one of them into tiny pieces.
Bits to scatter them on the floor.

For birds who visit us, sing for us.
After the rain has stopped,
The sun is just about to set, with its
Last rays falling on the leaves

Leaves of trees surround our house.
And we watch the stars shine.
Silence all around, with the
Bright moonlight falling on us.

All around us in the darkness,
As I tell you what I have read,
About the constellations above.
While you listen to me silently

I want to build a home with you.
A shelter with a porch outside,
A home filled densely with love.
A garden with all shades of life

POEM. 18

AWAY FROM HOME

(Home is that person, not a room, city, or state)

It's been a week, exactly seven days.
When we were together on the sand,
On the beach, states away from my
Room where I sit, alone, wrapped in
Blankets and pillows, staring at the,
Fairy lights that I hung on paintings,
Standing on tables, stools, and chairs.
Decorating higher parts of the walls.

They glow like warm stars in the sky.
I dream of decorating our little home.
with lights one day too, just warmer,
Brighter, your lap is softer than cushions.
When I would lay my head on your arm,
To sleep with my hair untied, flowing over,

Your bearded cheeks, all over your chest.
It's been a week, exactly seven days.

I would keep questioning myself if, at all
Your arm went numb because of the weight.
From the time that I have returned
I can't sleep like I used to, back then.
Because I've experienced what home is,
How could any place be as comforting as
Your arm, tell me, did it ever go numb?
By weight of my head that found home there

Home is no longer a room, city, or state
No longer these fairy lights and blankets
No longer the paintings hung on the walls.
Not the moonlight that shines so bright,
But, some golden sand on a beach, which
Has both our footprints, beautiful, discreet
A person, his arm, his cheeks, and chest.
It's been a week, exactly seven days

POEM. 19

SENSES

(Love impairs all senses)

Love is like a sheet made of
Translucency and deception.
Completely covering the eyes.
Top to bottom, like a curtain.
You cannot see the obvious.
Your decisions, all impaired.
Due to the lack of clarity in vision

It is like white noise that keeps,
Buzzing in your ears, like the
Sound of a bee near your hair.
You can't hear any other sound
Of the noble voices in your head,
Nothing else matters or makes,
Its way through your ear canal.

Every touch of love that you,
Feel on your body, arms, or legs
Face, chest, or the tender back
Passionate kiss on your lips.
Or, just a touch on your shin.
Takes away all other sensations
Only love is the feeling left.

Love is like the taste of warm,
Fresh apples and strawberries,
Filled and baked in a crusted pie.
Served with jam, cream, and ice
You can't taste any other fruit.
Or, even, think of the poison that
Resides for you inside its core.

It is like the smell of red roses.
Kept inside a vase, plucked, fresh.
With droplets of dew on them,
Every inch around you is filled.
With their sensual fragrance,
Decaying in this, you can't smell
The fire that burnt in the distance

POEM. 20

WARM NIGHTS

(Sleeping with your beloved)

Every night, when I lie down
To sleep after thinking of you
After imagining your face,
For an extra few seconds

I recall those warm nights,
When we were near each other,
When there was no distance,
Between the parts of our skin

When you would cover me tightly,
Our limbs would overlap.
And in the middle of the night,
When my eyes would open

I would kiss you, trying hard
Not to disturb you in your sleep,
And look at you for an extra
Couple of seconds, maybe

Also, rub my palm gently on
Your cheek, then, go back to
Leaning my head on your chest.
With those moments running

Running in front of my sleepy eyes.
I would slowly walk from the past.
To the future, and imagine all.
The nights that we'll have,

To spend time together in different,
Cities, wherever we travel
In different weathers, of all the
Seasons, in all the years to come

The nights that we'll have,
In the house, we build together.
Where, every night, we'll sleep
Like branches of trees intertwined

POEM. 21

FESTIVAL OF LIGHTS

(Celebrating festivals together)

I am so eager to celebrate,
The festival of lights, with you.
To decorate our little home,
With earthen lamps, candles
Placed in beautiful patterns,
To wear adorable Indian dresses,
May I take your help to drape?
The *sari* around my waist,
Look at us in the mirror.
To put candles on far to reach,
heightened places, with your help,
Make delicious sweets for you.
And make you eat lots of them.
Prepare for an entire week.
For this festival to arrive,
For the prayers, we would do.

I just hope we are together.
In the same place, dimensions.
When *Diwali* comes next year,
We would celebrate it together

POEM. 22

FLYING HIGH

(On the way to meeting your beloved)

I am sitting in the chair by the window
Travelling through the sky to meet you.
And I am not much used to flying high
Up above the clouds in the endless sky
Although, I am used to painting them.
Just the second air travel of my life.
I had forgotten how to board the plane.
Kept calling you at every single step.
Needed help to fasten up the seatbelt
During my first aeroplane journey, I wrote,
An article on how it felt watching sparkling,
Glittery lights on roads from the plane.
Lights inside doors of buildings, that
were viewed intermittently, as the clouds
Were playing hide and seek at night,
But, it's daylight this time, second journey

From above, large houses look tiny.
The clouds and huge farming lands,
Rivers and lakes penetrate their course.
Throughout, as I am still flying in the sky.
The happiness, this time, is different.
Almost elated and euphoric because,
At the end of this journey in the sky
I will get to see you, touch you, feel you.
I don't know how and will you be smiling
But, thinking about it again and again,
Brings a smile to my face, and that's how
I am living these moments, not admiring
The cotton clouds outside the window,
Or, the curly water bodies flowing below,
But, thinking of you smiling at the airport

POEM. 23

TIME STOPS

(Meeting after a long time, love in slow motion)

She entered the room
Filled with familiar faces,
Familiar figures around,
With just a few spaces,
Her eyes, searched for him
glanced in every direction.
Spotted him in no time
Walking towards her,
In a dark suit with a tie,
Heavy frills of her gown,
Of the colour of the wine,
flowed on the floor, like
Ripples in the ocean,
By a pebble thrown inside,
In all directions,
They were getting closer.

Each passing second,
She took a step and
A second step next
His tie fluttering over.
The fabric of his coat
As he moved, and she
Took another step, too.
Just a few feet left.
Some footsteps taken.
A feet apart, he stood.
Held her slender arms.
Pulled her closer,
Her waist to his chest.
His hands travelling,
Slowly, to her rosy face.
Figures Around them.
Cheering up romance.
He kissed her on the lips.
Her hands in his hair.
Time stopping, while
They taste each other.
Slowly, steadily, calmly,
Embracing the touch,
You meet your beloved.
After a wait of months,
Desire to drown in love.

in absolute slow motion
As if the time has stopped.
Feeling every detail,
The inner wave of passion,
The world sings, time stops
When you are in love

POEM. 24

PHOTOGRAPH

(Remembering nights spent together).

It was a golden moment.
We're lying closer than ever.
Flesh of hands, in touch
Fingers, entangled together,
The closest we have been,
Wanted to capture it, take a,
Mental photograph of that
Moment that felt like love
Keep it close to my heart.
Hide it somewhere, under
The pillow I use at night,
Or inside a vintage drawer.
Whose wooden key is mine?
Or, an old little pouch that
Hangs in my cupboard.
Behind the woollen coat,

Long, thick, impermeable,
Maybe, inside my journal.
Which, I open every day
To scribble, the feelings
You plant inside, when
I think of you, my love.
Or, inside the back pocket
Of my old navy blue jeans,
Somewhere away from the
Reach of any other being.
Reserve it in a brass frame.
Kept on the side table, near me.
Look at it whenever I wish
Feel the love in that exact
Moment, one more time.
And then, one more time.
And every time I look at it

POEM. 25

THE PACKAGE

(Sending love and letters)

I had something written for you.
In the inner folds of that paper
It was a long poem with words
Truthful, a string of white pearls,
Hopeful of the years to come.
Inside a package, that is travelling,
the distance between our bodies,
Oh! How much I had thought of
Meeting you in person today.
But, not just me, the parcel that
I sent, even that didn't reach
I will wait for a couple of weeks.
Till I reach you from this distant land,
And the poem written in that letter.
would meet you before me,
Accompanied by a few things,

Which, too, reside in the package.
Touched by me, will be touched by you.
The smell would remind you of me.
Till the time when we get to meet,
I am sending an overflowing,
Basket of love to your land.
Until I reach you in a fortnight

POEM. 26

TOMATOES

(Tasting new food together)

That was the first time,
You tasted bruschetta.
Bread roasted until the
Crust becomes, golden
Little square pieces of,
Fresh tomatoes, overlying
Healthy, soft, red, moist
Golden, the way you like.
Mist filled in the weather.
Sitting in front of me,
Telling me the feeling.
Of juice that swirled,
Flowed from tomatoes.
On your lips, tongue.
A perfect place to sit.

Next to your arms
Under clouds, travelling
Above us in the sky,
A meaningful meal to eat

POEM. 27

IGNORED

═══════════════════════════════════════

(Feeding with your hands)

Whenever, we go to a coffee house,
You don't sit next to me, closer, but
In front of me every day, every time,
I have to correct it, sit closer to you.
Next to you, where I can touch you.
And feed you little pieces of bread.
And jam with my hands, occasionally
Give you sips from my drink,
Touch your cheeks, fingers, lips.
Maybe you don't love me at all
Because, I remember, once you
Told me not to use the word 'love'
In my poems, I didn't write one
For a long time after that, until now,
Because I don't know how to,
Compose about anything else.

When I fall for you every day,
That's why I want to sit closer.
That's why I write about 'love'
Because I'm incapable of thinking,
Writing, of you, without love.
Everything starts and ends at that

POEM. 28

YOU FORGET

(Hesitant in love)

You forget one thing or the other.
Every time you come near me,
The first time you came in the rains
When the river was full,
Water melted from glaciers,
That flowed through narrow paths
Between mountains and hills,
You forgot to kiss me and said,
You were too shy to do that
Too shy to hold me by my waist
Squeeze it to the point where it,
Sends a chill down my spine.
I waited, you returned in the,
Month of autumn, when leaves
Orange, crimson, and mustard
All fall on the ground, where we

Step one by one, holding hands.
Just holding hands, you are shy.
Leaves crumbling beneath shoes,
Only sound in silence, you're shy

LITTLE THINGS

(Love is needed for the littlest things)

I am not afraid of living alone.
If I don't meet someone who
makes me feel loved and gives me
A reason to shine a bit brighter.
Someone who understands me,
to the deepest layers of my heart.
Someone who cheers me up,
But also accepts me at my worst.
I am ready to be alone if I don't,
Find a reason to love, though.
I firmly believe there isn't any,
Meaning of life without love.
But sitting on the rug at night,
buried inside the warm blankets,
Near the fireplace in winters,

With a bowl of berries and nuts, a
movie running in front of my eyes.
On the television set, I have been
watching it for a few minutes now
to silence the silence around,
That prevails in this woody house,
I fall asleep for quite some time.
Not knowing when it happened,
My eyes open abruptly in the
middle of the night, the world,
has slept, the movie has ended,
find myself sitting in a tilted pose.
In which I slept, numbed my toes.
It is then that I wish I had someone
whose arms would cover me,
From all directions, east and west
When I would sleep by accident,
After a tiring day on the carpet,
He would carry me to the bed.
Softly kiss on my pale forehead.
Keep moving his firm fingers,
In the spaces between my hair
as I go back to sleep in his lap
It is these tiny moments in life,

Which makes me want someone
Someone to love and to know.
How being loved would feel like
I need someone for little things

POEM. 30

FEELING LOVED

(Little things done by a beloved)

When someone says something,
Beautiful, about the way I am.
and I overhear their conversation.
With someone else, I feel loved.

When someone walks with me,
Down the corridors of our memory,
With the sun sinking below the
Horizon with us, I feel loved.

When someone cooks me dinner,
My favourite dish on the plate.
Feeling the taste of every bite.
Eating together, I feel loved.

When someone leaves a note,
In their absence, for me to read,
The concern in the words, the,
Messy handwriting, I feel loved.

When someone understands,
That I might be needing a hug.
Curls me tightly, which takes,
Away all the wrath, I feel loved.

When someone lends me their,
Jacket, on a cold winter night
The warmth it produces inside,
My heart and body, I feel loved.

When someone I fell in love with,
Looks into my eyes with passion.
Kisses my forehead with their
Soft lips, or cheeks, I feel loved.

Little things by someone matter.
Because we desire to feel loved,
Feeling loved matters; it's life
Feeling loved by you matters

POEM. 31

PIANO

(Loving the imperfections)

You told me one evening,
You were learning to play.
Play the piano every evening.
And you told me you would
Sing to me when you would
Have perfected a song about it.
I can't wait any longer,
I am ready to listen.
To you, all your songs,
The notes you play
Complete or part
All your imperfections

POEM. 32

OLD ROMANCE

(Old, childhood romance)

Have you ever thought,
What is the best thing
About old romances?

Apart from all the long talks,
That we did, sitting in the class.
With pages of a complicated,
Book kept open on your laps.
Paying just a little attention to the
Topics discussed in the subject.
Concentrating more on what's new,
In each other's life, with updates.

Apart from all the times, we
Went to have coffee together
At different, beautiful places.
That had fairy lights decorated,
Which brightened your skin,
And all the pictures you clicked,
Talking for hours about the past,
Present, future, or just silently sit.

Apart from the numerous letters,
We sent in the last few years,
Sometimes, sharing news that
Brought smiles to both our lips.
Sometimes, crying over issues.
That nobody else could feel,
Discussing our faults,
Successes, regrets, and fears.

Apart from the crisis phone calls,
That you made late at night.
Within a couple of minutes,
They were in front of your eyes.
There was always a comfort,
That they will be there with you.
No matter what, I will never judge
never leave, will never disappear.

Apart from all the memories,
You made with them back in time.
Which are trapped in the pictures
That fills the gallery of your device.
Which you can visit whenever,
And, wherever you miss them,
Because the past doesn't change,
It will remind you of the relation.

Have you ever thought,
What is the best thing
About old romances?

It is their pillars, based on trust
On boundless, everlasting concern.
On the fact that you were never,
Supposed to leave each other,
In the middle of the sea, aware
That they don't know how to swim,
Old romances are bottles of wine.
They keep getting better with time.
I have never had a sip, nor have you,
But, if it is like romance, it's true

POEM. 33

SEASHORE

(On the sand and in the waves)

The bright sun over the horizon
Ready to go beyond the ocean.
In the next few moments, while
We stand on the golden sand.
Sparkling, as the sunshine hits
Take a few steps back on shore
And again, come to the water.
That tickles our feet in motion
Not knowing where we belong,
Bare feet, touching the sand.
I want to swim in the ocean
With our warm bodies feeling,
Playful waves, as they cover us.
Feel each other as the sun sets.
But, we are not sure if we want
To leave the shore or stay, afraid,

Of losing the spiritual connection,
Of all these years in the past,
When we've stayed together,
That is limited to the land.
The ocean water is endless.
The ripples are huge and can drown
But, even if we keep walking,
Back and forth on the sand.
Someday, a powerful wave
Mighty, strong wave of love.
Would hit us, or maybe even
More threatening, one of us,
When it comes, the huge wave,
The sand won't sparkle,
It would burn our feet.
That's why I am afraid to go
Near the sand, near the shore

POEM. 34

TRAIN

(Parting at a railway station)

I have never found the railway station
As mesmerising as it was last Monday,
It was past midnight, and we had an hour.
A few moments to talk about the beauty
Of the sky, and few to walk under the
Moon and stars, which were shining brightly
I couldn't leave your hand because,
I knew you would meet me again after
A long time, even if it was less, I would
Never leave your hand. Pull you closer
Maybe, just try, because you are stronger.
We sat for some time on the metal bench.
I can dedicate poems and songs to you
The feeling that I had at that point of time,
I looked at you, lifting my face, in your eyes
for a few seconds, then your lips for a few

My gaze was fixed, but then I blushed.
I wish there were no people there, just us.
So, we could melt easily into each other
In the cold air that touched us whenever,
A train would pass by, and I would wish
Every time, your one gets, more delayed
So, we get a few more moments together
I usually write what I feel, so that it never
Goes out of my mind, gets trapped forever.
In words written in diaries, but what we had.
Even when it was just for a little time,
Even if I don't write or share about it at all,
The time that I had with you last Monday,
It will remain with me forever in my mind

POEM. 35

LITTLE LONGER

(Parting from beloved)

Next time, whenever you leave
Me at the airport after holidays,
Can we hug a little, longer?
More than the usual five seconds,
That is your stipulated time.
Maybe twenty this time, or forty.
or at least a minute long, or more.
So much that I could absorb.
A few particles from you,
Think of that minute every day.
From sunrise to sunset in the west
Hug so long that I could hide,
My tears are rolling down.
The edge of my cheeks can,
Bury my head inside your chest.
And will you just place a kiss?

On my lips when that minute ends.
Next time, can we just spend
One more moment before parting,
Because every second gives me,
A reason to smile multiple times.
In reality or dreams, wherever I am

POEM. 36

BAKERY

(Recalling evenings with the beloved)

Autumn leaves on the path.
Behind your wooden cottage,
Where I spent my evenings.
Sipping tea in your presence,
With some roasted biscuits,
From the bakery down the lane.
Where we went on weekends.
I don't remember its name

Orange, yellow, and brown.
Leaves falling on the road,
Swiftly moving away when,
breeze touches and flows.

We stepped on them while walking.
Listened to the crackling sound.
Thinking of the bakery's cake
I don't remember its name

Talking of all that happened,
In the years that passed by,
We reached the warm shop.
Decorated with golden lights,

A muffin sculpture on the top,
delightful fragrance in the air
Inside the bakery's glass walls,
I don't remember its name,
It was a long, tiring, busy week.
And I was lost in you, your talks.
Recalling that evening now,
You are nowhere to be found.

Can smell that fragrance again
Feel, taste, the cinnamon rolls
displayed on the counter of the
Shop, I can't remember its name.

I will go to the bakery today,
Buy some roasted almonds and biscuits.
But, where is the home you took?
Your cottage is empty, just wood

POEM. 37

LOOKING AT US

(Inside the water, under the sky, over the years)

Stop for a moment, a little while, I say.
Let's not swim, just rest on the edge.
This cold water is surrounding us.
Our bodies immersed up to our bust.

Put our hands outside, on the floor.
And inside us, let the fluidity soak.
Talk about everything that has changed.
Only a few have remained the same.

Remember, when we didn't know enough,
About people, places, and this world.
How innocent, how pure we were.
That's not how you survive on Earth.

The sun, the clouds, and the seasons are same
Rivers, roads, and winds are the same.
We were on the terrace of our flat.
Wrapped up in blankets, with coffee mugs.
Looking at the moon and glittering stars.
And yes, they were looking back at us.

We have fallen on roads that hit
Tore our clothes and gave bruises
Fought and stood up for ourselves.
Needed to stitch the lacerated ends.

Tears in eyes, filled with big dreams.
Wiped them away with the shirt's sleeve.
Thorns of fragrant, fresh, red roses
Hundred times, they pricked our hands.

Do you remember? Does it come to mind?
How we kept holding that rope so tight.
Hanging on for a little bit more.
It ended our search. We found our home.

Dreams, desires, and we have changed
Relations, emotions, sentiments changed
We are inside this cold water.
In strappy suits and swimming goggles,
Looking at the moon and glittering stars
And, yes, they are looking back at us

POEM. 38

CITIES

(Travelling together without planning)

I had already anticipated,
Even before meeting you,
It would be very tough
To go away after spending,
A couple of days with you,
In a city that was a stranger,
For both of us, but you still.
Made it feel like, Home
A Home that was far away.
From where we live now, or
Have lived in the past or,
Live in the years to come by.
I doubt if we would ever decide
To live in that city, but it would
Always be very close to me.
Because it was our first trip,

Together in a foreign land,
Yes, I was sad on returning
Because the trip ended a bit,
Too soon, too early, but we've
More cities to visit, to explore
Maybe I won't make plans.
Like every time before, hand
The roads would take us,
On paths, destiny has planned

POEM. 39

PHYSICAL

(The distance is only physical)

If only I could hold you tighter,
Stop you from going back.
Kilometres of land between us,
A vast, huge sky to travel before
I could physically reach you,
as in all the other ways,
Emotional or spiritual,
I meet you daily, each moment.
All the feelings that flood inside,
Me, at the thought of you, or in
A Biochemical way through all,
Hormones that run in my veins
When my mind thinks of you,
You are just inside me, there's,
Nowhere else do I have to go.
Search for you, no lands or skies

To be covered, to reach you.
Just the mere thought of you,
Where I then hold you tighter
In my mind, without any space
If only I could hold you tighter,
It would reduce physical distance…

RICE BOWLS

(Doing everything they like)

Someday, someone is going to
Sit next to you with a cushion.
On their back, and watch those
Romantic movies late at night.
When the world sleeps deeply,
The way you have wanted life.
They will agree to eat golden rice.
Mixed in peas, and other veggies
After they have been warmed,
In a designer pot, you brought,
From the Hills, two years back.
Someday, someone would sweep
Away the loneliness, without you.
Even noticing it a bit, in which,
You live right now, then your
Someone who stays right there.

Forever on the couch with a bowl,

And sometimes, you can both.

Share the rice from your bowls.

Or, feed them with your own hands.

Someday, someone would readily do.

All the things you want them to.

Not because they liked them, too.

But, of how much they love you

POEM. 41

ICED TEA

(Eating from each other's plate)

Oh, how much we loved!
Eating together, you would,
Order a mocha for yourself.
And iced tea for me.
Finish yours in minutes,
then, start sipping mine.
And you know, I didn't.
Like it at all, but it was,
Your way to irritate me.
Or maybe they really,
Made it extremely strong.
Frozen with tiny droplets,
Racing outside, the long,
Glass, from top to bottom.
Warming it, like the mocha
I get irritated on the surface.

But, inside, I melt like
Droplets racing from the top,
To the bottom of the glass.
Oh, how much I love
Eating with you, every bite…

POEM. 42

PEARLS

(Thirst for attention)

I wore every little piece
That would draw you to me.
Revealing parts of my skin,
Every pearl that wrapped,
Around my slender neck,
Had a purpose of being there.
The bracelet that I wore with,
Deep and dark wine shade
Which revealed all of my
Affection for you, all tissue
Of my back, filled up with
The desire of being touched.
Strapped laces that I wore.
For the first time in my life,
Because you had never seen,
My thighs before that night,

Every part of it was ready to,
Be unclothed to reveal what
They felt, and how nurtured.
They were, but still wanted.
A touch of you to fill up with.
Dense magic of liveliness
But you came, smile, slept.
Because you were tired,
Not realising that, I waited
All evening, for you to be near.
How I'd craved for attention.
Why, even the little pearl, bead
Hanging from my earlobe was,
Thirsty for your tender touch.
with which you would love,
And I stayed up all night.
Empty stomach, forgot to eat.
Your memories entangled me.
Maybe, tomorrow, you would
Not be that tired or occupied.
Or, maybe, come home early
And, for once in a while, look
At the inner parts of me,
Wrap me from bone to skin

POEM. 43

MIDNIGHT

(Wait all night for a glimpse)

And I waited more, more
Than the midnight looking
At the stars and moon,
Who remained by my company.
After you slept, you left.
And I wished for more, more.
You would return, maybe.
Before the sun rises

POEM. 44

A THREAD

(Feel that spark)

When we meet people,
Even when we don't touch,
Their skin, or hold their
Warm hands, filled with
Blood flowing inside,
We exchange energies.
We give and take vibes.
That stay with us for a,
Small or pretty long time.
Our minds have invisible,
Strings of the finest fabrics,
Strong enough, don't break.
By a subtle blow of wind,
We attach these threads.
Standing in front, without
Even touching each other,

And, when we are away
The threads communicate.
Receive, send energies.
Pull us a bit closer,
Reminding us of people,
Who have strings attached,
To our imaginative minds,
That is why, sometimes,
Even a moment spent,
With a person, with whom
Our soul is able to connect.
Seems like a comforting,
Eternal moment of a lifetime
A connection that wouldn't fade.
With changes in seasons,
Snowfalls or rains
A thread that connects to,
A soul in millions proves to,
Be stronger than the rest.
Brighter than the sunsets

POEM. 45

ASLEEP

(Not able to sleep)

Answer me, why did you sleep
Without talking to me today,
Because, when you go to that
Large bed with white sheets.
I stay up all night looking at,
The stars in the vast sky,
Thinking, if you thought what,
I was doing, while waiting.

While you were falling asleep,
I was thinking, dreaming of,
Singing you a song about,
How your eyes seemed to me,
When you look back at me,
About how everything that's
Inside me, has slowly started
Belonging to you, dancing.

Dancing to the tune of your,
thoughts, as you sleep,
The golden light that shines,
Through the window of your,
House from a lamppost on,
the empty and silent street,
I think about dancing with,
My feet tuned to your feet

Right next to the pebbles,
Scattered on the road outside,
And, I had thought I would.
Make coffee for us before,
We would slowly fall into,
The clutches of this night,
Like we did yesterday,
I just kept waiting, trying,

Not to feel lonely, gloomy
Hoping it was an accident,
Out of tiredness of the day,
Will you answer me in words?
Which would bring peace to,
My restless soul, all awake,
If I ask, why did you sleep?
Without me, alone, this night

POEM. 46

STAY

(Affection for the body, not the soul)

I could feel you with my thin fingers.
And rub your skin with their tips.
I could kiss you on your cheek.
Then, slowly travel to your lips.

Kissing them once and then again.
Feel your teeth biting my tongue.
I could play with your curly hair.
While you would untie, my bun

Bring my hands down to your neck.
While you move your hands,
We could do it all here and now.
All over my waist and on my back.

But, what about when we are done?
In this moment, under the bed covers.
When we have both felt the pleasure,
Would you still stay to fill that void?

Share with me your deepest desires.
And sing a melody in my ear.
Just curl your arms around my core.
Give me a place to hide, some more

Tell me your reality and dreams.
Will you listen to what my mind screams?
Unravelling the secret that we hold.
and make some more promises along.

Do we have something like this?
More than what our bodies, seek
Or, will you just vanish in the air?
Whenever I search for you in layers,

I want you to cover my body and soul.
Stay near me for a little bit more.
Just a shower or a candlelit dinner.
Forget these boundaries, be lovers.

Would you search for love in my eyes?
I want this answer, it's been a while
I will ask for it every moment, every time.
Whenever we come closer like this again

POEM. 47

YOUR EYES

(Something is stopping you from saying)

We talked about feelings buried inside.
Told each other how much we cared.
We did different things to portray our,
Desire and intimate affection for each other.
And now, we are silent, separated by time.

But, your eyes say something to me.
No other action shows that reality.
Actions speak louder than words. I agree.
But, your eyes reflect what words couldn't speak.
What your actions couldn't make me believe.

Last night, I saw the love in your eyes.
They avoided looking directly into mine.
Never looked into mine. I understand why.
They tell me the story of what you went through.
When you travelled this road alone,

They hold all the love you have for me.
I, eternally grateful for that, and will always be.
I think I am blessed more than anyone.
To have been loved in the purest ways,
To the extent that it consumes my soul,

Now, recall only the good places and days.
The incidents that made us both feel loved.
Let's forget the tough times that brought this,
Huge distance between us, where you avoid
Looking into my eyes, so just look for once.

I can read what they say, can't hide from me.
I am so delighted that I will always be,
A special person for you, you are for me.
Maybe you were right when you said,
We are soulmates, we are. Always will be

POEM. 48

LAST SUMMER

(Love, but can't have)

Sometimes, late at night.
When I sit with a few pens,
And scribbled journal inside.
A blanket next to a table lamp.
I remember, we met for a
Small span of six hours.
On a summer afternoon.
Had coffee and garlic bread.
And, even after all this time,
You are still on my mind.
I have written a handful,
Of poems that describe,
What I felt and feel now.
I have admired you,
learnt from you, being near,
Or, miles away from your town.

It was a month ago when,
We sneaked out to spend
Having counted six hours, we had
If only we could buy more time,
I would have stayed.
Longer with you, maybe
The entire, blue starry night.
And one more day after that.
Maybe a few more days.
That would fulfil my hope.
Of having you in my life,
Only if I could buy some
Days filled with moments,
Of places and love of the past
I wonder what magic would,
Have happened if you were
With me for a much longer,
An extended period of time.
I could keep writing all my
Life with your memories

POEM. 49

WHERE ARE YOU

(Where did you go?)

I thought you were playing.
Lawn tennis, a little longer.
You had left in the evening.
To the court, I don't know
How far have you gone now?
I had been waiting in here.
Hours of intense silence.
Thinking about the things,
I would tell you when we,
Talk like every other night.
Little did I know you won't,
Knock at my door all night,
Just end the day uncertainly.
But, how would it be when
I wouldn't be able to sleep
Without looking at your face,

Endless reasons that run,
through my restless soul,
But, if you would appear
In front of me, anytime.
Of this long night, bring,
Bring oxygen to my lifeless lips.
What could be so harsh?
That doesn't let you say
Don't want to imagine
Even the worst reasons
That might lie behind,
Your non-responsiveness,
How could you just vanish?
In thin air, when the moon
Is clearly visible in the sky.
I hope there's some reason,
Enough to make up the,
Desire for togetherness

POEM. 50

FULL STOPS

(Never ending love)

I don't like full stops
I don't like ends;.
Also, I think every end,
Also, it is a new beginning.
Every letter that I write to you,
Every song that I sing for you,
Would only be a precedent,
Would only be an octave to,
A fresher, upcoming letter
A new verse of the song,
To be written,
To be sung
Love has no full stops
Love has no end

POEM. 51

COLD HANDS

(They feel pity, but can't love you back)

You know that too
It was an awkward moment.
Maybe one that could have,
turned into something deeper.
You were standing in front of me.
I was sitting on my scooter.
The golden light particles from,
The street lamp fell on our faces.
I didn't want our conversation to end
Why couldn't it continue?
Like the cold breeze that flowed,
It was time for me to leave
I extended my hand in front of you.
For an essential touch before,
You leave the city and go away from me.
for a very long and uncertain period of time

You placed your hand on my hand.
My hand was much colder than yours.
As I was driving sometime before,
to reach you in the garden outside,
You touched my hand with one of yours.
You noticed it was cold,
touched it with your second hand.
For a little while, our hands were in touch.
My cold skin melting by the warmth of your hands.
A moment with no explanation.
You were pressing my hand
In the grip of your palms for a, moment
The moment felt as vast as the sky.
We saw into each other's eyes.
I don't know what felt different
There was one moment of silence, where
Hands were in touch, and eyes were locked
with the only light source being the,
lamppost behind your back and then,
You left my hand with me, keeping it just
A fraction of a second longer in front of you,
in the hope that you might hold it again
But, equations have become complicated
and emotions have been felt way too much.
In the recent past, not now, but maybe
Sometime in the future, after years

You would hold it in a similar manner.
Just to warm it, and then not leave it,
Like you did tonight,
We would come closer in the,
Moments that follow and hold each other,
not let even a particle of light from,
The lamppost behind you gets in between.
It would be dark and warm.
It would be a string of moments when,
We would embrace each other.
Maybe in the future, it happens to us.
Maybe some other night

POEM. 52

YOU DON'T EXIST

(Need love to remove confusions)

If only you were there,
To tell me what to do,
When dark clouds of,
Uncertainty fog the eyes,

To narrate the stories,
That you experienced,
Because you're older
And, history repeats.

To hold my hand,
Tell me how to choose,
Between the sparkle,
And the dull, but useful,

If only you were there,
To listen to my pain,
All that I have to say,
loneliness that stays,

To console me that
It will be fine soon.
And you will always,
Be there, night to noon.

But you don't exist,
Your place in my life.
Is just a huge void.
I don't know what to do

DOORS OPEN

(They won't come, but you wait)

My eyes, waiting for you.
To get inside, through
The glass door beside,
The flower vase that,
Had roses decorated,
With fresh droplets of,
Scented water sprinkled,
I knew you didn't know,'
About me being there.
But, even then, a part
Of my soul, that always
Wants to be with you.
Wished you would come.
Inside, through the door.
And every time it opened,
The edge made a sound.

My eyes would look up.
I knew it wouldn't be you,
But still, each time,
My eyes would look up.
All around, to search you.
In the crowded place,
Where doors would open,
Close every now and then

POEM. 54

SET YOU FREE

(You leave for good)

Early morning, I rushed.
Outside the corner room,
Walking fast through,
the staircase, corridors,

Knowing completely that,
I might regret the decision.
Of leaving you alone, later,
In fact, I wanted to regret.

To be able to, undoubtedly,
accept that, if something,
was ever real, it was us.
kept walking fast, running.

Through the main gate,
While you slept inside,
blankets on the mattress,
unaware of the fact, future,

When you wake up,
won't find me next to you.
I will be far away, realising.
I did wrong, very wrong.

But, I can't stop, turn now.
It's for the better, the best,
Me staying away from you,
Is the best thing I could do.

Sometimes, you have to
leave people, even when
You love them the most.
You've to set them free.

Even if it destroys them,
Or, rips their heart apart.
For it'll just be a moment,
Spent in pain, separation,

When it is over, moment,
In the pages of the past,
I will be an old memory.
But, I would still love you.

Though, away from you
Still filled with regret,
Early morning, I rushed
I'll regret it my whole life

POEM. 55

REST

(Beloved is lost)

Let me tell you how much,
I miss being with you lately.
I wrote you a lengthy letter.
A week ago in the beanery

Where I used to sit alone,
After my evening classes,
Ordered almond cookies,
Sipped glasses of cold, latte

Last week, when I went there
A pen and a pile of papers,
On the crimson couch, where
I wrote a lengthy, long letter.

Date, time, and place at the top.
Beautifully scribbled, your name.
Then, everything I have ever
Thought in my mind to say,

Hands of the clock kept moving.
So, did my fingers with the pen.
On the papers that now know,
More than you at, present

My mind thought faster than
The pen could write, words
Emotions flowing in my vessels.
The pen twisted and twirled.

Kept writing there for hours.
The ice in the latte, had melted.
And I saw the sun, about to set.
through windows in the West

Sat there for the longest time.
In a few months, always alone,
At the bottom of the letter,
Lots of love, I wrote for you.

It is safe with me in my bag.

It will wait until we meet next.

Or, should I post that letter?

Above the clouds, where you rest

POEM. 56

STILL DO

(Everlasting love)

I still love you, though, I'm not there
Next to you, with your arms around
My waist is peeping through the shirt.
Bordered with embroidered laces,

I still love you, though I'm not there
To tell you the tale of incidents that happen
During the day, when the sun shines and
How I fall asleep at night in moonlight.

I still love you, though I'm not there
To rub my hands on your shoulders,
Whenever you feel a little low,
Shed tears, only need me by your side.

I still love you, though I'm not there.
To smile with you in the sunshine,
When you open your eyes after the,
Warm and satisfying sleep at night.

I still love you, though I'm not there.
To say, to express it in front of you
Like, I used to do daily several times.
Looking into the depth of your eyes,

I still love you, though, I'm not there
Not so courageous and outspoken.
At this point in time, I could let
You know how I feel, without you

POEM. 57

BURNT BY LOVE

(Gamble everything for love, get burnt)

I am ready to give up.
On a lot of things, only
If I get the love I have,
Dreamt of since I was,
A little girl with bows,
Bright coloured, tide in
The locks of my hair,
But then, I wasn't aware.
Of inner desires and,
Deeper emotions that soil,
The idea of being loved,
And loving again, after
being wounded, burnt,
But, I am ready to get
severely hurt, just to feel
what I have dreamt of

POEM. 58

CLOSED DOORS

(Love of dominance and secrecy)

I wonder what happens,
Behind the closed doors,
Which separate us from,
The reality of faces,
expressions that live on them,
when hidden inside
Away from the outside,
rest of the World, that
Wears a mask to hide.
What they think, desire,

But, behind the closed
Strong doors made of,
Dominance, captivity,
No mask is ever worn.
Fears, doubts lie naked.

On pale, distorted faces,
Wounds open, bleeding.
Because no one watches,
I wonder what happens,
That needs to be hidden

POEM. 59

SECRET

(Lust, not love)

You kissed me in silence.
When nobody was watching,
When nobody was aware,
What was growing between, us
When we were exchanging,
Letters written with words of
Love?
Lust for each other?
Which made me feel as if
You needed me more than
Any other thing in the world.
You missed me in silence,
Told me when we met.
When nobody was watching,
We were living a story
That nobody knew, heard

We were loving in silence.
You kissed my lips and bit.
Taking away my pain.
Accepting me with flaws,
Wrapping me in your arms,
We captured those moments.
Even talked about them later.
But, when I asked you if
You loved me the way I did.
Ready to love me when we,
Weren't hidden, doors unclosed
You went away, and I was alone.
Left in the desert of memories.
Haunting me all day, all night.
You didn't love me in silence,
You destroyed me in secret

POEM. 60

CAGE OF LOVE

(Love destroys us)

It bruises our skin.
And splits it open
Uncovering a pile
Of emotions that
Were hidden there
Unsaid, unexpressed
It rips the muscles.
Breaks the bones
It kills us, hitting
Like falling stones,
From the sky do
We cripple and
Crawl on the floor
Can't stand more
Love weakens us
Drains us of all

Lymph and blood
We lie down still
Can't sit anymore.
The pain, deadly
More than our
Capability to hold
But we still do
Every day we do
Trap ourselves in.
The cage of love

POEM. 61

LAST KISS

(It's your last meeting)

I knew that it was going to be the last kiss.
That I gave you on your cheek, while you
Pretended to be asleep, lying on the bed.
Under the sheets, curved up on one side.
I didn't want it to be the last and hoped
You would hold my hand and pull me closer.
To yourself, and stop me from going away.
I wanted you to show me, describe in words.
Actions, how much you wanted me to stay
I was craving that sort of desperation.
From you, the one I loved every moment.
I wanted you to hold my wrist and kiss me.
Back, but on my lips, and stop the time.
Nothing happened; it was all in my mind.
So, I knew as soon as I turned back, that

It was our last, my last kiss on your cheek.
The last touch that made me feel the love
Residing inside me, for someone I knew.
It was the last, though I didn't want it to be

POEM. 62

A BROKEN HEART

(A broken heart still knows how to love)

It is not easy to love a
Heart that's been broken
Into irregular little pieces.
Scattered away from the
Pure body, where it lived.
Waiting to be gathered.
By someone who could,
Find a home for them.
When it rains or storms,
Pick each one of them.
One by one, with hands.
Collect in a basket of,
Warmth and tenderness.
Stick them to a shape.
Heart that could feel again.
Because, if it was broken,

It must have been loved.
It must know how to love.
The pieces must know how.
Love the broken heart, pieces.
to make it recall the love

POEM. 63

NEVER SAY

(Not showing when love hurts).

Some of us never say,
Never let it come on.
The soft surface of our,
Tender lips, even once,
But, we still get blown.
By the swirling cyclone,
Which, in our mind, flows.
Terrible winds and storms,
We never say, but feel.
Understand every little,
Intent and detail, all,
Words forming a string,
Most of us never say,
We try to hide it under the
Opaque surfaces of our skin,
Express less, but crave for,

You every moment of the day.
I say that less, mostly just,
Open the voice notes.
That you had, sent me
And listen to them once,
Then, again and again

POEM. 64

WHENEVER IT HURTS

(Not talking about love when it hurts)

We all do it all the time.
Whenever it starts hurting,
Whenever the tears are on the verge,
of being thrown out of our eyes,
resting at the brim of the eyelids,
we do it,
We change the subject.
We think that may be because,
We don't talk about it,.
we would forget it
But do we really?
We try to avoid eye contact.
when it happens,
Looking in all directions,
Except for the eyes of the person,
we are hiding from

We just change everything.
from the aura of the air around us,
to the tone of the conversation,
Everything needs to be changed.
as soon as possible to stop it
To stop the tears from flowing out,
on our cheeks, and let them have
the alternate pathway of sliding down,
swiftly, peacefully, through the
nasolacrimal duct inside our nose.
so that nothing is visible on the outside.
We have succeeded in hiding our emotions.
Once again, we have done it

POEM. 65

ANGUISH

(Separate, but still craving for love)

I am waiting for a moment when,
It would happen one more time.
Covered sparsely, moss-green bushes.
In the isolated ground at night,
I know you seemed too tall,
It was difficult for me to reach.
After raising my toes on the grass,
Your cold, frosty, flawless lips
But, I know it will happen again.
When we find a place to sit,
Nothing would seem so far,
Neither the night nor the union,
Of our intimacy-craving, anguished
Dry as a bone, waterless lips

BURNING WOOD

(Harming yourself for love)

I've spent nights there.
On dirty, moist bedsheets
Carelessly put alongside,
The logs of wood burning.
On cold, breezy winter nights
I've cried, opened up in
most of the ways possible,
Ended restrictions and broken,
All boundaries, without thinking.
Night after night, my love for you,
was so true, so concerned about you,
Only you, not me. I stopped thinking.
About the consequences of sleeping in a
Closed room with burning wood

POEM. 67

LEAVING

(Leaving for my beloved)

You can leave material things.
You can leave going to places.
But, can you leave people?
Will the memories leave you?
For the people you love.
It is that easy to ignore.
The eyes you knew deeply.
To cross them on streets,
which you walked together,
Surrounded by tall trees,
Orange leaves on both sides.
Can you leave people who,
Once there were alongside.
When you laughed or cried,
On that street, you walked.

For new people you know?
For new people, you love?
And even if you leave, people
Will the memories leave you?

POEM. 68

AUTHORITY

(You love them despite their wrath)

Why do you have to shout at me?
Why do you have to raise your voice?
Is it authority over my body you seek?
Or, control over my mind that thinks.
Does this anger fill your nerves?
A subtle way to depict your tough love?
Is it what I get in return, the wrath, pain?
For the selfless love that fills my heart

POEM. 69

VIOLENT TOUCH

(You love them, despite their violence)

The sad part was
I wanted you for
Physical intimacy
Because I needed
Someone to curl
His arms around
My waist filled
With red bruises
Painted on my body
Every night by you
I know you don't
Care even a bit
About my swollen
Thin fingers which
Are difficult to move.
You would never

Feel what I felt for.
You all night, day
But I want to stay
Beside you for a
Little while, because
I want someone
To hold me tightly
I don't seek any
Emotions or concerns,
If you would have
Had them inside you.
Would have come for,
Once to see my back,
Contusions red, blue
And I don't want to
Speak even a word
Just want to lie alone.
Witness the silence,
Touch of another body

AFRAID OF LOVE

(Afraid of loving because of the past).

Every time, I am left broken.
After a lover leaves me, alone
With all the memories in my
Hand that slowly percolate
Through the cells of my skin,
Just to haunt me every time.
I think of getting attached.
I firmly affirm myself, not
To fall in love with someone,
Another soul that comes across,
And feels like home, intimate.
Little home, muddy, damp floors
But, is it really possible to
Not slip on the wet, sticky
Uneven base with legs.
Shivering, haunted by the past?

FRAGILE

(A fragile love)

I have sacrificed a lot.
To keep you in my life,
It has taken away bonds.
Made through years
Which I thought were not.
Possible to easily fade.
Then, go on and break.
But, the truth is here.
Every connection, new, old
Is replaceable, is fragile
It's just a matter of time.
Of the way you look at it.
Emotions that arise,
Chemicals that run through,
Your mind and veins.
They can break everything.

Even the toughest of all.
People are fragile
I admit the relations.
Of the past have to wither.
To build something new,
That smells fresh, alive.
But, how do we know?
What happens with time?
Everything that has life,
Comes with limited time.
The past was, the present is
Even future that is yet,
To take place, is fragile

POEM. 72

BREAK

(Love not strong enough),

Somewhere I knew
We would break
Like every other thing,
That breaks within
Seconds or seasons
Everything that is
Not strong enough
And so were we
Not strong enough
I am just grateful
Saved from storms
Torrential rains and,
Waves, I was mature.
Enough to realise
That it was indeed
Soon, going to break

POEM. 73

SHINING

(Love that is fading with time)

Will it keep shining?
Always
Or, is it just waiting?
To get covered with dust.
Slowly
Getting buried under rust.
That eats away light.
Layers of unbreakable iron.
Tough
Will it keep shining, or
With time, something
Stronger will end every bit.
Nowhere to be found?
Ever

POEM. 74

WRONG THINGS

(When love is morally wrong, ethically wrong)

Wrong things are tempting.
We do them not to hurt.
But, to satisfy the Demon,
That hides deep within us.

We know it is not correct.
Not validated by the crowd.
But, we can't live without
Doing things that are wrong.

Maybe we don't find them
Outside the circle that holds,
All the sweet and beautiful.
Deeds that people tend to do.

For some, the circle is larger.
Some stick to its boundaries.
Some hover around the,
Edge, moving out and in

Wrong is not universal.
It is still correct for some.
Or, few, or correct for just
The demon living inside us

STOP WRITING

(Getting over unrequited love)

I have to stop writing about you.
Because, the more I imagine you.
The more I fall for you, violently.
Every morning and every night,
Adore you from a distant sight.
Knowing that I can't have you,
Stab myself with my own hands.

I have to stop writing how I feel.
In letters that I never post,
Poems that fill the pages of my,
Diary that I won't let you read.
But, they describe you in the most
Beautiful ways, so tempting, that
Anyone falls for you, reading them.

I have to stop being obsessed.
With you, with all that you do.
With your mighty, strong arms,
Because it's like living in a dream.
That would never come true.
It would create more pain inside.
My heart that aches every night

I have to do myself this favour.
Not harming myself anymore.
Not endlessly thinking about you.
I have to try not to dream like,
I have dreamt for the last few months.
Tried and failed, but maybe,
Someday, I wouldn't fail anymore

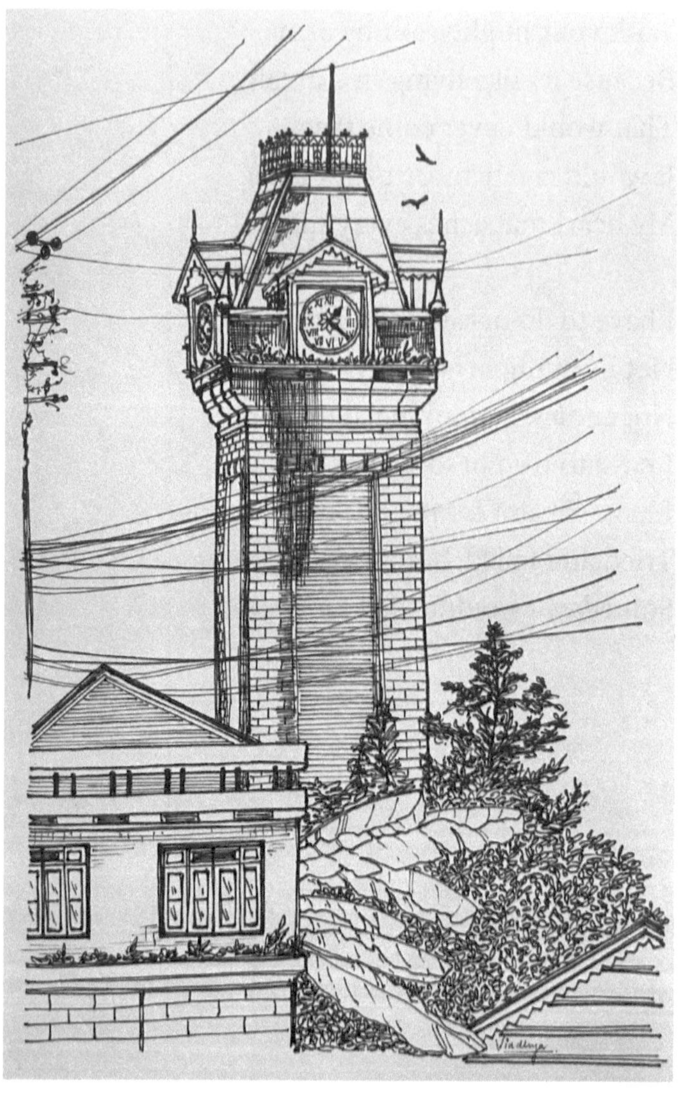

EPILOGUE

Dear beloved,

I remember writing my first letter to you. I didn't use the full stop after the last word of the last line of the poem.

You said, "Put a full stop here," folded the piece of paper and inserted it inside the wallet, which you inserted in your back pocket.

"I don't like full stops," I said.

"Then mark three of them there," you said and smiled...

ACKNOWLEDGEMENTS

I thank my parents for making me who I am and for always teaching me the correct things. They have witnessed me going through the toughest days of my life and have felt my pain in their hearts. I think, as we grow older, we start understanding our parents better.

I thank Garima and Arjun for being with me throughout time, no matter how dominating I would get as an elder sister sometimes. I remember locking my door from inside the room to write in silence and isolation. They haven't disturbed me at all (thanks to my mother for keeping them out).

To my cousin, Siya, for being the first and honest listener of scattered parts of the manuscript, and more for being someone in whom I could see scattered parts of myself. I had realised this inheritance years back. However, it was a discovery for her as she listened to the poems in this book.

To both my grandfathers, who are no longer in this world but loved me more than any other child of my generation. I will always keep the memories fresh.

To my entire family, the one in which I was born, and the one of which I have become a part of, for being a comfort zone and always believing in me.

To Banaras Hindu University, my Alma mater. It has been a home to me for nine years. To all the people I became friends with who have helped me understand love better just by being in my life. To all those who have taught me about love, intentionally or unintentionally.

And finally, I thank my husband, Vipul, who is exactly what I wished for. I can't be more grateful to life. He is the exact man of my dreams who seems to have borne out of one of those. All the poems about the comfort provided by love in this book were written for this man. But he has successfully been able to not get even the least emotional or romantic about any of it. Yes, a person like me, hopelessly romantic, could wish for a man as practical as him. And get one too…

2025, a book about loneliness.

UNTITLED

It was raining
On the buildings
On the trees
And on the road
The road, covered with
Earthworms and twigs,
From branches of trees,
Which hung on the road.
From up above
Lifeless, they had fallen.
Broken from their roots,
Road was wet with the,
Water of the rain
It was night
Dark everywhere
The earthworms looked,
Like twigs moving
Here and there
The twigs looked like.

Silent, motionless earthworms.
I was afraid that those,
Might get inside my shoes.
Earthworms, not the twigs,
More afraid of the living,
Than the non-living.